# Become a Professional Repair Expert in 30 Days

# Terms and Conditions

# **Table Of Contents**

# Foreword

- 4 -

There is usually a set style of tools that is suitable for anyone wanting to be a handyman. This is quite basic and should be very easy to acquire.

# Become A Professional Repair Expert In 30 Days

# Chapter 1:

*Essential Tools For A Professional Handyman*

---

# Synopsis

Good tools can make the difference between a well done and easy experience and a frustrating and poorly finished job. This is one of the secrets of a good handyman, as matching the correct tools to the job is part of getting the best results and an overall satisfying experience.

# The Basic Tools

The following are some of the tools that should be part of the tool kit of a professional handyman:

•	A 16oz hammer is perhaps the most important tool to have. However, the weight of the hammer can vary according to the individual's preference. Getting one that has a rubberized grip would be even better.

•	A saw is another handyman tool that is considered important as it is able to do all the cutting jobs that may be required. A saw with a cross cut should be able to handle most jobs. Try to keep the length and size smaller as this will ensure it is easy to store in the kit.

•	Screwdrivers that come in a set of about 6 pieces will be adequate to handle almost any job. Here too, getting the ones with a rubberized grip would be a better option to look for.

•	Tape and a stapler are both tools a kit cannot do without. Although these items may seem simple, they are able to keep almost anything is place either temporarily or permanently.

•	A drill with a good variety of bits will facilitate any handyman job very well. Getting both the cordless and the electric drill will be ideal for the handyman who needs the flexibility of both types.

- Level bars are also another essential item, as they are a good measuring gauge to ensure all the fixtures and items are placed in a level and balanced manner.

# Chapter 2:

*Top Skills 1: Woodworking*

---

# Synopsis

Woodworking can be approached as a hobby or as a profession; either way, working with wood has been an exercise almost everyone has participated in at some point in their lives. With the correct tools and some knowledge, woodworking can be a very fulfilling experience.

# Woodworking

Most of the tools that are used for woodworking are sharp and potentially dangerous, therefore care needs to be exercised whenever such tools are being handled. Taking the appropriate precautions will limit the chances of injury. Experienced woodworkers will be able to difference between the various types and qualities of wood and also their most suitable uses. Knowing the advantages and disadvantages of certain woods is helpful to ensure the appropriate choices are made for the particular job at hand.

Having a suitable amount of space to work with is also another point to consider, as limited space will eventually contribute to mistakes and injury occurring frequently. There should be adequate space for the relevant tools to be laid out for use and also space for the assembling of units that may be rather big and bulky. Without such space allowances, getting the job done well will be a challenge which could contribute to a lot of stress.

When it comes to tackling joints for woodworking, the use of nails, screws and other mechanical fasteners, may not be always necessary. In woodwork exercises there are a lot of other types of joineries that can be applied and such methods produce equal quality work.

Woodwork does not always mean working with wood to produce pieces such as furniture, cabinets, frames and other more conventional items. It can also be a form of wood turning which would involve the designing and making of items such as bowls, decorative pots, pens and decorational art effects.

# Chapter 3:

## *Top Skills 2: Plumbing*

---

# Synopsis

Plumbing can almost always be a rather complicated and difficult task to tackle. Therefore, it may be a better option to hire a professional to get the job done correctly and to ensure a suitably lasting effect.

# **Plumbing**

The expertise of a handyman, when it comes to handling plumbing jobs, includes fixing water leaks in kitchens, bathrooms and any other areas where water is the cause of the problem. For a seemingly simple task like changing a faucet, especially if the faucet chosen is a fancy and more decorative styled piece, hiring a plumber to install the unit maybe better than actually trying to tackle the task without any expert knowledge. In almost all instances, what may seem like a simple and straight forward task to the layman, is actually a rather complicated plumbing issue that would be best handled by a professional handyman with plumbing expertise. This is also the most cost effective and timely way of handling any plumbing problem.

Most basic plumbing tool kits would include the following:

•	Plunger – this tool should be able to fix most minor blockages without much fuss. It can be used in bathrooms, toilets and kitchens where the blockage is not extensive or serious.

•	Hand auger – this tool is usually used when the plunger is not able to deal with the blockage adequately. The design of this tool enables it to be stuffed down into pipes and drains, to unclog any blockages.

•	Wrench set – these tools help to deal with leaks and loose pipes and the selection should include a basin wrench, a pipe wrench and an adjustable wrench.

• Tongue and groove pliers – these tools are also known by their brand, which is Channelocks. This tool is used to tighten, loosen, grab, twist or hold anything related to a plumbing problem.

# Chapter 4:

## Top Skills 3: Basic Electronics

---

# Synopsis

With a little bit of trained knowledge, it is not that difficult to understand the basics of electronics and their connective uses. Having a basic knowledge of how circuitry boards work will help you to have a better picture of the overall electronics experience. All electronics people should know the various connotations involved in this line, before actually attempting to handle any electric related problems.

# Basic Electronics

The following are some elements connected to the electronics theme:

•       There are basically two types of electrical signals, which are AC and DC. With the DC style, the electricity flows in one direction between the power and the ground where there is always a positive source of voltage and ground source of voltage.  The electricity is defined as having a voltage and a current rating which are then depicted as Amps.

•       The circuit is a complete and closed path through which the electric current flows between power and ground, thus an open circuit would work in the opposite way of where the flow of electricity is broken.

•       The resistance feature is an important part of the circuitry as it ensures the electrical flow is being channeled and used, otherwise a short circuit will occur. Short circuits occurring are bad as they can cause severe damage to the electrical item and also cause fires and explosions. Therefore, ensuring the electrical flow is never wired directly to the ground is very important.

•       Understanding and choosing between series and parallel is essential in deciding its appropriateness for the intended electoral item.

•       Resistors are in place to help reduce and balance the flow of electricity. They come with different wattage ratings, which are low voltage DC circuits of ¼ watt resistors.

•       Capacitors are components that store the electricity and then discharge it into the circuit when there is a disturbance which results in a drop in electricity.

•       Diodes are components which are polarized and they only allow electrical current flows in one direction. This is useful when there is a need to check for a flow in the wrong direction.

# Chapter 5:

*Top Skills 4: Advanced Electronics*

---

# Synopsis

There are several different elements that are usually covered in the advanced electronics platform. Exploring these features will allow anyone to make the appropriate choices for their needs.

# Advanced Electronics

The following are some of the areas where advanced electricians are prominently featured for their individualistic contributions:

•	Project definition – at this point, the idea behind the need for the advanced electrician contributions is decided. Here the various features are matched and chosen.

•	Cost analysis – the advance electricians tools will be able to provide the relevant assistance for development and identifying new possibilities where advanced electronics can be effective.

•	There is also a positive contribution where the advanced electrician will be able to assist in any probable applications for the architecture and design for any product or endeavor.

•	Software development – advance electronics can also contribute in this area, where the embedded programs can have better hardware installed, which produce more efficient and functional codes for the equipment.

•	Advance electronics can also contribute to the products interfacing with computers and where the software functions systematically to ensure the hardware accepts and understands it.

With constant advancment electronics progress, there is always a possibility of new products and inventions being developed. These developments are meant to enhance the general working of everything connected to the comforts of human life. There are a lot of areas where advanced electronics can apply to the common person and these may include hiring the services of a handyman who has such capabilities, to address problems such as home repairs, remodeling and maintenance. Having the services of a handyman, who is well versed with the advanced electronics platform, will help to ensure all problems are accurately and effectively solved.

# Chapter 6:

*Protect Yourself From Injuries*

---

# Synopsis

Injuries are a common occurrence when dealing with handyman work. However, some measure can be taken to minimize the injuries and its frequency.

# Stay Safe!

The following are some of the areas where caution should be extended to help minimize the possibility of injuries:

•	The handyman should always try to avoid using the table saw fence for crosscuts. This is especially so when making the mistake of starting on wood that is still wet or a bowed and twisted piece of lumber. Using a fence as a guide for cross cutting is dangerous and a better alternative would be to use a miter gauge or build a cross cutting sled.

•	Removing the blade guard is another action that should not be practiced, although a lot of handymen seem to disregard this very important precaution. Failing to observe this will certainly result in injury, should any distractions occur while using the blade.

•	Holding the board with the hands directly behind the circular saw, is also a folly often taken for granted. Using a temporary nail or clamp is a much safer option.

•	Placing the hands or using the hand to grip near the area where nail guns are about to be used is also another mistake that is often made. The hand position holding the board should not be too close to the nail gun. Handling nail guns carefully is very important, as a lot of accidents occur with careless misuse. Disconnecting the hose and keeping away from the trigger is very important.

•       Careless use of knives or blades is also another common cause of injury. Therefore, when using either of these, the handyman should keep focused and not allow any distractions to complicate an already potentially dangerous situation.

•       Using the relevant protective gear for the face and eye area is important. Safety goggles and face shield should be a standard piece of protective wear used by the handyman.

# Wrapping Up



Tackling any task is certainly achievable for the common handyman. With the help of these tips you could be handling issues around the house like a professional. Much time and money can be saved by doing things yourself. Along with this comes a sense of pride from doing something with your own hands. So why keep paying others to do your handy work who are likely doing a poor job? Get out there and do it yourself, I know you can!